Pigs Say Oink

A FIRST BOOK OF SOUNDS

A Random House PICTUREBACK®

Pigs Say Oink

A FIRST BOOK OF SOUNDS

by Martha Alexander

Random House New York

Farmyards are noisy in the morning. While the animals
wait to be fed, they make all sorts of sounds.
Cocka-doodle-doo crows the rooster on the fence.
Pigs say *oink! Oink! Oink!* Little piglets squeal.
Cluck, cluck, cluck say the chickens as they peck
for corn. Baby chicks say *peep, peep, peep.*

After the farmer milks the cows,
he leads them to the pasture.

Cows say *m-m-m-o-o-o-o!*
Little calves say *m-m-m-a-a-a!*

Baa-baa-baa say the sheep, grazing in the meadow.

Baa-baa-baa! The lambs call to their mothers.

Horses neigh. Colts do too.
Clop-clop, clop-clop go the horses' hoofs.

Hee-haw! Hee-haw! bray the donkeys as
they crunch on apples in the shade.

Ma-a-a-a says the nanny goat.
Ma-a-a, ma-a-a say her kids.

Hungry turkeys say *gobble, gobble, gobble*
as they run to be fed.

At feeding time the ducks come running.
Quack! Quack! Quack! Peep-peep! Squawk!
Rat-a-tat-a-tat! A woodpecker pecks at the tree.

The rabbits in their hutch are quietly
munching on carrots and lettuce.
The catbird in the tree calls *mew-mew*.

Caw! Caw! Caw! shriek the crows as they fly
around the scarecrow.
Katydid says the katydid on a blade of grass.

The wind blows. The tall grass rustles.
Bobwhite calls the quail, hiding in the field.
Bobwhite! Bobwhite!

Plop goes a big stone—into the water.
Splish, splash go the frogs as they jump in.
Big bullfrogs croak. *Jug-a-rum, jug-a-rum.*
Rib-bit, rib-bit call the little ones.
Swish, swish, swish goes the windmill,
turning in the wind.
The bumblebees go *buzz-buzz-buzz.*

BUZZ-Z-Z-Z-Z-Z-Z-Z

RIB-BIT

RIB-BIT

CLICK-CLICK

The freight train whistle blows. *Choo-choo!*
Chug, chug, chug goes the engine as it pokes
along the tracks.

Clang! Clang! The bell at the railroad crossing rings.
A passenger train zooms by on its way to the city.
Clackety-clack-who-o-o-sh go the wheels.

Loud noises, screeches, clatter, and sirens—
there are so many sounds on the city street.

It's lunchtime at the city zoo and all the animals are waiting to be fed. Monkeys chatter. Elephants trumpet. Lions roar. Hyenas laugh. Bears growl.

Birds squawk. But mother giraffe softly chews her cud.
Arf! Arf! Arf! bark the seals, bobbing their heads to
catch a fish.

Pr-r-u-m! Pr-r-u-m! Beat the drum. *Toot! Toot!*
Blow the horn. The rhythm band is playing music.
How many musical sounds there are!

The grandfather clock goes *tick-tock, tick-tock.*
The cuckoo in the cuckoo clock goes *cuckoo! Cuckoo!*
Clocks and watches everywhere are ticking off the hours!

Purring! Barking!
Hissing! Panting!
Meowing! Growling!
Whining! Yowling!
Cats and dogs make
all these sounds.

Honk! Honk! Honk! call the geese as they fly
high in the sky. The dog howls at the moon.
Ice skates go *click, click, click* on the frozen pond.

Someone falls down . . . *Boom!*
The owl in the tree says *who-o, who-o, who-o!*
Swoosh goes the sled, gliding down the snowy hill.

Sh-h-h-h! Don't make a sound.
Everyone is sleeping . . .
except the mouse.